D0570973

WHAT DOES THE PRESIDENT DO?

BY KATHLEEN CONNORS

Gareth Stevens
PUBLISHING

CRASHCOURSE

Please visit our website, www.garethstevens.com. For a free color catalog of all our high-quality books, call toll free 1-800-542-2595 or fax 1-877-542-2596.

Cataloging-in-Publication Data

Names: Connors, Kathleen.
Title: What does the president do? / Kathleen Connors.
Description: New York : Gareth Stevens Publishing, 2018. | Series: A look at your government | Includes index.
Identifiers: ISBN 9781482460513 (pbk.) | ISBN 9781482460537 (library bound) | ISBN 9781482460520 (6 pack)
Subjects: LCSH: Presidents--United States--Juvenile literature. | United States--Politics and government--Juvenile literature.
Classification: LCC JK517.C66 2018 | DDC 352.23'0973--dc23

First Edition

Published in 2018 by
Gareth Stevens Publishing
111 East 14th Street, Suite 349
New York, NY 10003

Designer: Samantha DeMartin
Editor: Kristen Nelson

Photo credits: Cover, p. 1 Orhan Cam/Shutterstock.com; series art MaxyM/Shutterstock.com; pp. 5, 7, 9, 11, 29 (Johnson) courtesy of the Library of Congress; pp. 8, 19 Bettmann/Bettmann/Getty Images; p. 13 (map) Electric_Crayon/DigitalVision Vectors/Getty Images; p. 13 (photo) Jewel Samad/AFP/Getty Images; p. 15 Bloomberg/Bloomberg/Getty Images; p. 17 MCT/Tribune News Service/Getty Images; p. 21 Jim Watson/AFP/Getty Images; p. 23 Stan Wayman/The LIFE Picture Collection/Getty Images; p. 25 Diana Walker/The LIFE Images Collection/Getty Images; p. 27 Jason and Bonnie Grower/Shutterstock.com; p. 29 (Clinton) Larry St. Pierre/Shutterstock.com; p. 30 Everett Historical/Shutterstock.com.

Printed in the United States of America

CPSIA compliance information: Batch #CS17GS: For further information contact Gareth Stevens, New York, New York at 1-800-542-2595.

CONTENTS

Words in the glossary appear in **bold** type the first time they are used in the text.

THE CHIEF EXECUTIVE

The president is the head of the executive branch of the US government. The executive branch makes sure the laws of the nation are followed. The president leads this branch through the many jobs he or she must do.

MAKE THE GRADE

The judicial branch of the US government has to do with the courts and is headed by the **Supreme Court**. The legislative, or lawmaking, branch includes Congress.

PRESIDENT WILLIAM HOWARD TAFT

WHO CAN BE PRESIDENT?

In order to become president, a man or woman must be at least 35 years old. He or she must have been born in the United States and have lived in the country for at least 14 years.

MAKE THE GRADE

Presidents come from many backgrounds. Today, they're commonly lawyers who became **politicians**. In the past, they've been farmers, schoolteachers, and military leaders.

PRESIDENT
ULYSSES S. GRANT

7

US presidents serve 4-year terms, or periods in office. They can only serve two terms. This limit was set by the Twenty-Second **Amendment**, passed by states in 1951. Many presidents have served two terms.

MAKE THE GRADE

President Franklin D. Roosevelt was elected four times! When he died during his fourth term, Congress believed it was necessary to limit future presidents' terms.

**PRESIDENT
FRANKLIN D. ROOSEVELT**

9

Running for Office

Presidential **candidates** spend time before the **election** spreading their message. They travel around the country giving speeches and meeting **citizens**. Candidates for president are commonly part of the Democratic or Republican **political parties**.

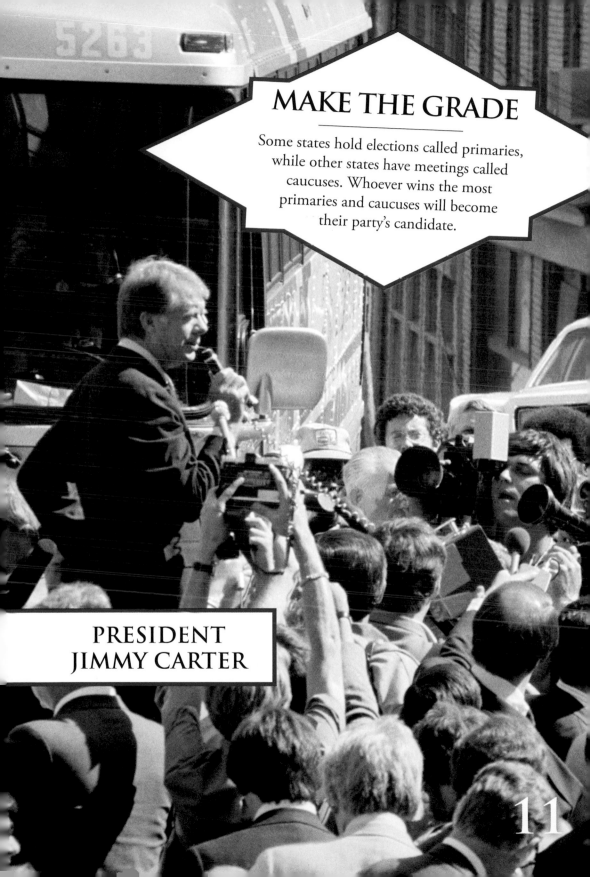

MAKE THE GRADE

Some states hold elections called primaries, while other states have meetings called caucuses. Whoever wins the most primaries and caucuses will become their party's candidate.

PRESIDENT JIMMY CARTER

To become president, a candidate must win the most electoral votes in the election. Each state is worth a number of electoral votes equal to the number of **representatives** it has in Congress. Of the 538 electoral votes, a candidate needs 270 to win.

MAKE THE GRADE

Most states award all their electoral votes to the candidate who receives the most individual votes in that state.

ELECTORAL VOTES MAP

WA 11
MT 3
ND 3
MN 10
ME 4
OR 7
ID 4
WY 3
SD 3
WI 10
MI 17
VT 3
NH 4
NY 31
MA 12
NV 5
UT 5
CO 9
NE 5
IA 7
IL 21
IN 11
OH 11
PA 21
NJ 15
RI 4
CT 7
DE 3
MD 10
DC 3
CA 55
AZ 10
NM 5
KS 6
MO 11
KY 8
WV 5
VA 13
NC 15
OK 7
AR 6
TN 11
SC 8
TX 34
LA 9
MS 6
AL 9
GA 15
FL 27
AK 3
HI 4

13

POWER FROM THE CONSTITUTION

Once in office, the president has certain powers given by the US **Constitution**. As head of the executive branch, the president is the commander in chief of the armed forces. This includes the ability to **pardon** someone.

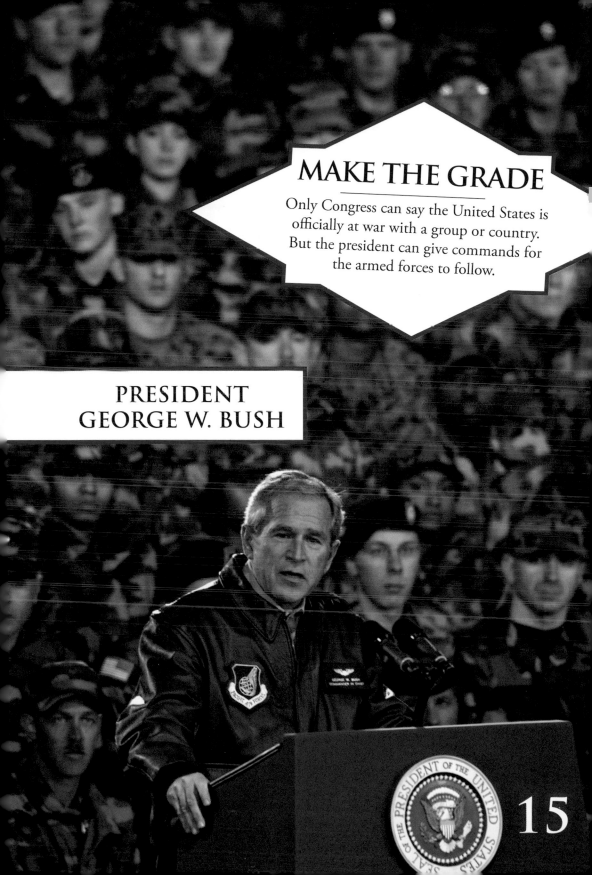

MAKE THE GRADE

Only Congress can say the United States is officially at war with a group or country. But the president can give commands for the armed forces to follow.

PRESIDENT GEORGE W. BUSH

15

Another major job given to the president by the Constitution is the power to appoint, or choose, some government positions. The president appoints justices to the Supreme Court, **ambassadors**, and more. The Senate has to approve, or agree to, these appointments.

JUSTICE
ELENA KAGAN

MAKE THE GRADE

The president appoints a group called the cabinet to help run the executive branch. They head government offices that take care of parks, collect taxes, and more.

The Constitution states that "from time to time" the president should tell Congress the "state of the union." It's become a yearly speech the president gives to both houses of Congress. He or she often states present thoughts and plans for the future.

MAKE THE GRADE

The three branches of the US government are meant to check and balance each other. No one branch should be more powerful than another as a result.

PRESIDENT
GERALD FORD

19

The president has the power to make treaties, or agreements, with countries and groups around the world. The Senate approves these, too. The president is also the face of the United States, representing the country to other world leaders.

MAKE THE GRADE

The president works to keep up friendships the United States has around the world. Dinners and other events at the White House are often given in honor of world leaders.

PRESIDENT BARACK OBAMA
AND VIETNAMESE PRESIDENT
TRAN DAI QUANG

21

IT'S THE LAW

The president balances Congress's power by choosing whether or not to sign a bill into law. The president has 10 days to sign a bill into law. The president can also veto a bill, or stop it from becoming law.

MAKE THE GRADE

The president has an agenda, or subjects he or she wants addressed. The president works to get Congress to vote on bills important to this agenda.

PRESIDENT LYNDON B. JOHNSON

A veto isn't always final. If two-thirds of both houses of Congress vote to override the veto, the bill passes without the president's signature. Congress may also change a bill somewhat and try again to get the president to support it.

MAKE THE GRADE

A pocket veto happens when a session of Congress ends during the 10 days the president has to sign a bill—and he or she doesn't do so. The bill stops there.

PRESIDENT
RONALD REAGAN

25

Next in Line

If the president dies or chooses to leave office, the vice president becomes president. The Constitution doesn't state this directly, only that the office of the president "devolves" on, or passes to, the vice president. The Twenty-Fifth Amendment made it law.

VICE PRESIDENT JOE BIDEN

MAKE THE GRADE

In the Constitution, the vice president's only job is to be the head of the Senate, where he or she would cast a tie-breaking vote if needed.

27

Impeachment

The president must follow the laws of the United States. If it's believed the president has done something wrong, the House of Representatives can impeach him or her. No president has been removed from office after being impeached.

MAKE THE GRADE

"Impeach" means to charge an official with a crime while in office. Only President Andrew Johnson and President Bill Clinton have been impeached.

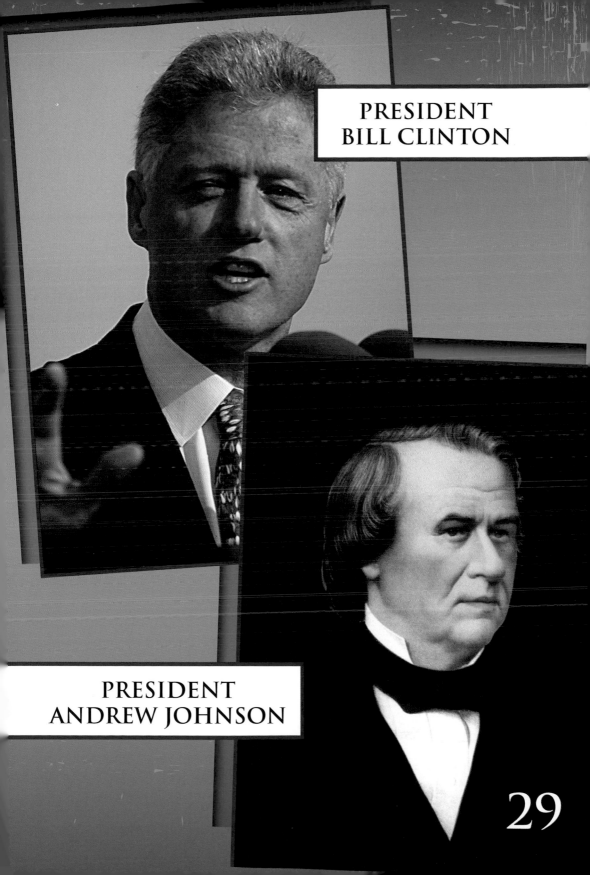

PRESIDENT
BILL CLINTON

PRESIDENT
ANDREW JOHNSON

29

WHAT DOES THE PRESIDENT DO?

- appoints ambassadors, justices to the Supreme Court, cabinet members

- represents the United States to world leaders

- gives the State of the Union address

- leads the executive branch

- signs bills into law

- vetoes some bills

- makes treaties

- is commander in chief of the armed forces

PRESIDENT
THEODORE ROOSEVELT

GLOSSARY

ambassador: someone sent by one group or country to speak for it in different places

amendment: a change or addition to a constitution

candidate: someone who runs for a public office

citizen: someone who lives in a country and has the rights of one who lives there

constitution: the basic laws by which a country or state is governed

election: the act of voting someone into a government position

pardon: the act of excusing someone of an offense

political party: a group of people with similar ideas about how government should be run

politician: a person who runs for or holds a government position

representative: a member of a lawmaking body who acts for voters

Supreme Court: the highest court in the United States

FOR MORE INFORMATION

BOOKS

Meltzer, Brad. *I Am George Washington*. New York, NY: Dial Books for Young Readers, 2016.

Porterfield, Jason. *What Is the Executive Branch?* New York, NY: Britannica Educational Publishing, 2016.

WEBSITES

Congress for Kids: Executive Branch

congressforkids.net/Executivebranch_index.htm

Learn all about the governmental branch headed by the US president.

Publisher's note to educators and parents: Our editors have carefully reviewed these websites to ensure that they are suitable for students. Many websites change frequently, however, and we cannot guarantee that a site's future contents will continue to meet our high standards of quality and educational value. Be advised that students should be closely supervised whenever they access the Internet.

INDEX